Planting Seeds

What the Word of God Does for Our Lives

Lenora Turner

authorHOUSE®

AuthorHouse™
1663 Liberty Drive
Bloomington, IN 47403
www.authorhouse.com
Phone: 1 (800) 839-8640

Published by AuthorHouse 05/30/2019

ISBN: 978-1-5462-4735-7 (sc)
ISBN: 978-1-5462-4734-0 (e)

Library of Congress Control Number: 2018907160

Print information available on the last page.

Any people depicted in stock imagery provided by Getty Images are models,
and such images are being used for illustrative purposes only.
Certain stock imagery © Getty Images.

King James Version (KJV)
Scriptures were taken from The King James Version of The Bible - Public Domain.

This book is printed on acid-free paper.

To My Family,

My First Ministry

Introduction

The fight is not between us it's over us. Who will get possession of our minds to do whosoever's will. The more we receive of the word of God the more we become like Jesus and the more we receive of the things of this world, its thoughts and ways of living the more we become an enmity to God. No servant can serve two masters either he will hate the one and love the other; or he will hold to the one and despise the other. Ye cannot serve God and mammon. **Luke 16:13**.

We as Christians have been bought with a price. Purchased with the precious blood of the lamb for we were captives to another master. Now that we have been freed our will is now to the one who has set us free. That we are now no longer and still are not of ourselves. But by the word of God which is the will of the Father, has penetrated us by his son Jesus Christ through the Holy Spirit, which is his word. God wants us to be willing and obedient children unto Him.

We must allow the abundance of the spirit to begin to come alive in us so that the promises of his word will become manifested in our lives. Gods' word is action. Just as in the beginning he spoke his word, and let there be light, it did just what it was told to do. So if we allow the word of God to be spoken over our lives, over our situations, over our families, over our children, the awesomeness of God would begin to set captives free, loose those that are bound, heal those that are sick, and would begin to open those port holes of heaven and pour out the wisdom, knowledge and understanding of His ways and will. The more word of God we have the better we are equipped to do his will and to allow his will to be done in us. What we failed to realize is that the things that come against us is by our own actions and reactions, whether it be of good or evil. We think that the circumstances which come about is because of someone else's fault. But, once we have been taught what thus saith the Lord the spirit of the enemy comes upon us and instead of us using the weapons given us, the word of God, we begin to use our own carnal minds which is evidently the wrong route to take. But if we would just hearken to the voice of God by those that have the rule over us, life would be a lot easier to live.

The Sower

There is a familiar parable in the Bible of **THE SOWER.**

As we read it we see all the different ways in which the seed was received into the earth. It was not freely received at times as it was freely given. This example was given to us because these are the ways in which Gods' word is being received in the Christian Family.

Genesis 1:11,12 And God said, Let the earth bring forth grass, the herb yielding seed, and the fruit tree yielding fruit after his kind, whose seed is in itself, upon the earth: and it was so. And the earth brought forth grass, and herb yielding seed after his kind, and the tree yielding fruit, whose seed was in itself, after his kind: and God saw that it was good.

Have you notice that there are some fruits that have no seeds in them? Grapes and watermelons to name a few. Well I just want you to know that is not how God planned things to be, everything God said He made is to yield seed after his kind.

Genesis 1:26 Let us make man in our image, after our likeness: and let them have dominion over the fish of the sea, over the fowl of the air, and over the cattle and over all the earth and over every creeping thing that creepeth upon the earth. Then God blessed us and said to be fruitful and multiply…**Genesis 1:28** I do not believe He was talking about giving birth in the natural. I believe He was speaking about the continuance of our growing in the spirit to exercise our dominion over everything in the earth. That is doing

1

what **John 15** says in staying connected to Him we would be and do just what He had said we would do and be. Instead we choose to eat fruit from another tree so now that seed has been planted in us. But God knew that so now he has given us a way of escape by being born again that the first seed that was planted can be revived and take its rightful place in us to be who God has called us to be from the beginning. **Jeremiah 1:5** Before I formed thee in the belly I knew thee.

God's word is seed to who we really are a spirit, housed in flesh, the dust of the earth.

What we have to first realize is what purpose Gods word is for in our lives. That ye put off concerning the former conversation the old man, which is corrupt according to the deceitful lust; and be renewed in the spirit of your mind; and that ye put on the new man, which after God is created in righteousness and true holiness. **Ephesians 4:22-24**

In **John 1:1, 14** says In the beginning was the Word and the Word was with God and the Word was God. And the Word was made flesh, and dwelt among us.......So what did the word come to do? To be an example. An illustration of a general principal of behavior that is to be imitated. Now we know that there are two types of examples in the Bible, those of good and those of evil. Those that obeyed and those that disobeyed. But we as Christians are to focus our minds on the things that are good. What a valid point the focusing of our minds. Let this mind be in you, which was also in Christ Jesus. **Philippians 2:5**

The mind is a terrible thing to waste and it is so true. But for the most part the majority of us have done just that. We have lived our lives mostly for the adversary, which is how we have wasted our minds. The things of evil that we had conceived and conjured up in words and deeds profited us nothing, if anything we were cutting our life span shorter and shorter, for the word of God says, that the wages of sin is death but the gift of God is eternal life. Not just a natural death but a spiritual death. This is why Jesus came. He had to preach the gospel to the poor he had to heal the broken hearted, he had to preach deliverance to those that were captives, he had to give sight to the blind and to set at liberty those that were bruised, he had to preach that now is the time to come on the Lords side for the kingdom of God was at hand. Now these things were at no way easy to do because he was pulling the covers off the adversary. He was exposing the devices in which the adversary was using to keep the people of God blinded and in bondage. Jesus was bringing light to the darkness of the world. Giving people a choice on whether or not they wanted to stay in the darkness of the world which is sin or come to the light and live which is Jesus.

So now Jesus is God in the flesh by the Word which is God Himself, then as we begin to receive the word of God, He begins to manifest Himself in us and through us by His Word.

Sounds easy enough right

The Ground

Question. Where does the different grounds come from in the planting of seed?

Answer. When there is no understanding of the purpose of the word of God in our lives.

Revelation 2:7......he that hath an ear, let him hear what the Spirit saith unto the churches. The spirit is the Word of God and the churches are us the Christians. Now before I go any further I must clarify what Christian means. Christian means to be anointed followers of Jesus. For Christ was not Jesus' last name "Jesus the Christ" meaning Jesus the Anointed One.

In **Mark 16:15-18** Jesus had commissioned his disciples to go out into the world and preach the gospel to every creature. Those that would believe signs would follow them and the works that they did would be done in his name and the works that they did do were the same works Jesus did when he walk the earth, but these things would not happen until they did what was said in **Luke 24:49** And, behold, I send the promise of my Father upon you: but tarry ye in the city of Jerusalem, until ye be endued with power from on high. On the day of Pentecost in the upper room the Holy Spirit was received by those that were in the upper room which is the promise. They now possessing the Holy Spirit which is the third person of the Trinity. God, Jesus and the Holy Spirit all three are one. So now that they had received the Holy Spirit the same works that Jesus did, Peter and John also were given the same opportunity by the Holy Spirit in healing the lame man. And that was how the name Christians was form because the works of Christ were being performed. That is why it is so important that we not be so quick to say I am a Christian, because the world is watching us and if the works are not being performed in our lives if we do not bare the fruits of Christ we become a false witness of Christ to the world. Hearing what God is saying to us through and in his word we have to get an understanding of what the Word of God does for us in our lives. The word of God when it is received should bring to mind **I SEE**. Not with natural eyes but with spiritual eyes.

The word comes to point out the things that are not like God which is sin. So now you say, what must I do to get rid of this sin? Your answer lies in **Acts 2:38**, Then Peter said unto them, Repent and be baptized every one of you in the name of Jesus Christ for remission of sins and ye shall receive the gift of the Holy Ghost.

In our repentance we are asking Jesus to forgive us for the sins we have committed in words and deeds. Well some of us will say I've never lied, I've never smoked, I've never drank, I've never did drugs........but the word of God says, For all have sinned and come short of the glory of God.**(Romans 3:23)** Repenting is not something you do and take lightly, as though you were just having a casual conversation. Repenting comes with a sorrowful heart and the knowledge of committing yourself to doing the will of the Father. Next comes the baptism which also is a marriage. The baptism symbolizes the death and burial of Jesus in the tomb. **Romans 6:3, 4**. In **Matthew 28:19** Jesus commissioned his disciples to teach all nations and be baptized in the name of the Father, and of the Son, and of the Holy Ghost. **John 10:30** says I and my Father are one. **John 5:43** says I am come in my Father's name.......... So if Jesus and the Father are one, and Jesus has the name of his Father. What name are we to baptize in? **JESUS**. That is the name of the Father that is the name of the Son and that is the name of the Holy Ghost.

Neither is there salvation in any other: for there is none other name under heaven given among men, whereby we must be saved. **Acts 4:12** Where does the marriage part come in so you say? Just as a woman takes on the name of her husband in marriage. What name have we taken on in the baptism? **JESUS.** So now that you have been born again the ground is now being prepared to receive the seed, the word of God.

God has given to me **I C C C C** (I see) and each of these letters reveals what Gods' word does in our lives.

The Seed

The letter I is for **Instruction**, commandments, knowledge. A direction for procedure, a particular course of action. **Deuteronomy 5:1** Hear O Israel the statues and judgments which I speak in your ears this day, that ye may learn them and keep and do them. **Proverbs 3:5, 6** Trust in the Lord with all thine heart and lean not unto thine own understanding in all thy ways acknowledge him and he shall direct thy paths. In Deuteronomy God had given Moses the commandments in which the children of Israel were to abide by, and in doing so, they would get the victory over their enemies they would never lack of anything and they would reap where they had never sown. These are the promises of God that he has proclaim to us in our obedience to him.

Now we also know what happens when children are disobedient. **Chastisement.** Correction. To subject oneself to moral or spiritual discipline. **Hebrews 12:6** For whom the Lord loveth he chastenth and scoureth every son whom he receiveth. **Ephesians 5:17** Therefore be ye not unwise, but understanding what the will of the Lord is.

There should be no doubt to what the will of the Lord is for that is the first thing that he has given us, his instructions, and commandments. Just as a natural Father will set certain rules and guide lines in his home for those that are living there. So likewise does our heavenly Father. Just as our natural father chastises us for our disobedience. So it is in the case of our spiritual Father. Just as the natural Father knows of the dangers of the outside world that he wishes to protect his children and love ones. How much more do you think our Heavenly Father cares for us for it is he that has been here since the beginning and will be here in the end. **Revelation 1:8** I am Alpha and Omega the beginning and the ending, saith the Lord, which is, and which was, and which is to come, the Almighty.

His desire is that none of us should perish. So as he is correcting us through the chastisement of his word we are to learn, that what we have done and are doing is not the will of God.

We as Christians must pay attentively to the word of God. We are to study to show thyself approved unto God......**2 Timothy 2:15**. Studying Gods word shows and tell us all of what Jesus was and all that he did and didn't do and all of what was done to him.

And we still say to one another I want to be more like Jesus, but what we fail to do is to study the word to see all of what it cost to be Jesus.

Jesus was a man of meekness and humility. He was a man under authority, who knew authority and was authority. He was a man who did no sin neither was there any guile found in his mouth. He was talked about, scorned, reviled, rejected, hated without a cause, but not once did he retaliate. He was stripped of his clothing, spitted upon, hair torn from his face and mocked. But the most devastating things that were done to him was the thrashing thirty-nine times with a whip that actually had torn flesh from his body. He then had to carry the cross in which he was to be placed on. They then nailed his hands and feet to the cross using large iron spikes and upon his head were place a crown of thorns. Last by not lease a sharp sword was taken to pierce his side.

So what are we complaining about when things are not going the way we want. So what if a brother or sister lies on us, so what if when you come into the mist of people and silence befalls and they begin to disperse, so what if you're the only one that says Amen when the word is going forth, so what, so what. It was the Pharisees and the

Scribes, those who had the law, those that went to the temple that wish to see harm come to Jesus.

Why? Because they were not living what they were teaching and professing to be. They were also using the law to please the flesh. To look important to the people, and to keep the people oppressed. This was what Jesus came to reveal to the world. And just as they came against Jesus so shall that same spirit comes against us in those that are around us today.

Jesus never told us that it would be easy, but he did say I'll never leave you nor forsake you. God has given us the weapons to combat the enemy and that is his word, which is Jesus himself. The battle is not ours it's the Lords'. Now as we begin to abide in the word and that word abides in us persecution will come but we have to remember that the word of God is also a comfort.

Comfort, a resting place, a place of peace, to console, a place of contentment. **Psalm 55:22** Cast thy burden upon the Lord and he shall sustain thee, he shall never suffer the righteous to be moved. **Hebrews 13:5, 6** Let your conversation be without covetousness; and be content with such things as ye have for he hath said I will never leave thee nor forsake thee. So that we may boldly say, The Lord is my helper and I will not fear what man shall do unto me.

We are witnesses unto God. He has chosen us before the foundations of the world. He has made known unto the world that he is God. He has made known that he is the Creator. No one and nothing was here before him. Yea before the day was I am he: **Isaiah 43:13**. He has made known his deliverance power. He has taken us out of our wilderness, just as he did for Moses and the children of Israel in taking them out of the land of Egypt. **Exodus 13:9...** for with a strong hand hath the Lord brought thee out of Egypt. He has made know that he is the Redeemer. **Colossians 1:14** In whom we have redemption through his blood, even the forgiveness of sins: He has made known that he **is Holy. 1Peter 1:16** Because it is written, Be ye holy; for I am holy.

God word is self-explanatory. God says what he means, and means what he has said. Now that he has redeemed us we have to boast of Gods marvelous works which he has done in our lives and in the lives of others. Not only in our talk of God but how we carry ourselves and how we live. To show the world that we are proud to be called children of the living God. We are to show the world how well our Father takes care of us, to show the world how well our Father provides the things that we need to survive, to show how all our needs are being met by our Father, without us putting our confidence in what man can do for us. To show how whenever we need him he's always there and never fails us no matter what the situation is, no matter what the problem is, he's just a prayer away.

We are to place our lives in the Lords' hand. He is our burden bearer. When man has forsaken us the Lord said....lo, I am with you always, even unto the end of the world. Amen. **Matthew 28:20**. Being that we came to the Lord just as we were, there are of course things which are not of God, so therefore there's work to be done to cultivate the ground.

Construction. To build up, to tear down, to put together and to rearrange. **Hebrews 4:12** For the word of God is quick and powerful, and sharper than any twoedge sword, piercing even to the dividing asunder of soul and spirit and of the joints and marrow and is a discerned of the thoughts and intents of the heart. **1 John 3:8** He that committeh sin is of the devil: for the devil sinneth from the beginning.

For this purpose the Son of God was manifested so that he would destroy the works of the devil. Jesus left his home in glory to do the will of the Father. Jesus being God himself denied himself by having compassion on his creation. He sees the weakness in us. He sees that we were not capable to fend for ourselves against the wiles of the devil.

God knows that he has the power and the authority that we needed so he devised a plan that the same power and authority in which he has would be imparted to us by Jesus Christ his only begotten son through the Holy Spirit.

Now that we have been born again which is a transformation from the way we use to think, speak and live to a way of living a God fearing life, which is pleasing to the Father. That the things that we use to do, we have no desire to do them, and the people we use to be with to do those things we have no desire to do with, and the places we use to go with those people to do those things we have no desire to go anymore. Our minds have been renewed we have received the gift of God, the Holy Spirit, which is he himself. **Philippians 2:5** Let this mind be in you, which was also in Christ Jesus:

The word of God also **Controls**. It conforms, leads, guides and causes us to comply. **1 John 2:27** But the anointing which ye have received of him; abideth in you and ye need not that any man teach you: but as the same anointing teacheth you of all things and is truth and is no lie and even as it hath taught you ye shall abide in him. Once we were born again of the spirit we are no longer of ourselves, we must remove us, we, I, you, they, and them out of the way so that Gods' will, will be done in our lives. And to do that we have to take Gods word at face value, because what he said and says is what he meant and means. Jesus took the burden of our sins to the cross, then he says for us to come to him all that labor and are heavy laden, he will give us rest. To learn of him and to take his yoke which is easy and his burdens which are light. So now if Christ took all the sins of the world and paid the price for them which was his life, and passed all the test of temptations of the world, and he says to give him all of what we may be going through. We now have the Holy Spirit, and it's now no more us that lives but Christ that lives in us. There's nothing for us to worry about or to concern ourselves, all we have to do is be obedient to the word, worship, praise, and give thanks and allow ourselves to be available at all times to be used by God. On that third day Christ rose with all power in his hand, so if we have him in us the Christ in us is going through, he's already went thru and passed all the trials and temptations. Right now he's just being re-examined in us. Then said I, Lo, I come (in the volume of the book it is written of me,) to do thy will, O God. **Hebrews 10:7** This is the mindset that we are to have in serving God in the righteousness in which he has already map out for us in his word.

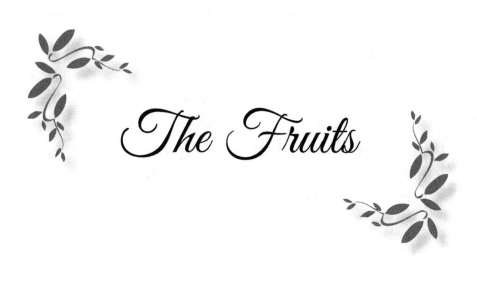

The Fruits

Just as in the days of John the Baptist, the men and woman of God have been preaching the word of salvation. For us to prepare ourselves for the return of Our Lord and King. To get our houses in order so that the King of glory can come in. Now that the sower (the preacher) has prepared the ground (the saints) and the ground has received the seed (the word of God) and the rain (trials) and sun (tribulations) has come and gone, the fruits (characteristics of God) are now to be yield up. **Galatians 5:22,23** But the fruit of the Spirit is love, joy, peace, longsuffering, gentleness, goodness, faith, meekness, temperance, against such there is no law. These are now the attributes in which we as Christian children of God are to be living in as well as walking in, why because we are our Fathers seed, begotten by the gospel, and this is his character. Just as Jesus told the Jews, if ye were Abraham's children, Ye would do the works of Abraham. **John 8:39** Let us just characterize each of the fruits of the Spirit that we may get a better understanding of the way we ought to be living as Christians. For a good tree bringeth not forth corrupt fruit: neither doth a corrupt tree bring forth good fruit. For every tree is known by his own fruit.... **Luke 6:43, 44**.

<u>**LOVE**</u>, charity, the thinking of others needs before ourselves. For God so loved the world, that he gave his only begetton Son.... **John 3:16** this is the love in which God showed toward us

even though we did nothing to deserve it that he look beyond all our faults and saw that we were in need of a true Savior.

JOY, the center of delight.....for the joy of the Lord is your strength. **Nehemiah 8:10**. The very thought of all of what the Lord has done for us should bring about joy. For all that the Lord has done and is doing and is going to do is all unconditional, meaning there is nothing that we have done that merits the favor in which God has and is given to us.

PEACE, a calmness, a freedom from worries, troubles, fear, a state of mind. **John 14:27** Peace leave with you, my peace I give unto you: not as the world giveth, give I unto you. Let not your heart be troubled, neither let it be afraid. We all know that no matter how good things seem to be going in the world there will never be peace until **Revelation 21:4** And God shall wipe away all tears from their eyes; and there shall be no more death, neither sorrow, nor crying, neither shall there be any more pain: for former things are passed away.

The peace that Jesus is speaking about is that peace, we have within knowing God has all things in control. That no matter what the situation may present itself to be God has no problem handling it. Is there anything to hard for God? I know that there's not, how about you!

LONGSUFFERING, patient. **Romans 2:7** To them who by patient continuance in well doing seek for glory and honor and immortality, eternal life: People are not always going to be in sic with you, so just as Jesus has been patient with us and still is, so are we to have patience with others. There are times when we ask ourselves when are my children going to listen to me, when are they going to get on the right track, when are my family members going to get it right with God, when, when, when. Do you realize how many times God has said that since man was created and made in his image? How many times he has said that about us before we came into the knowledge of him, and even now there are still things that we are still wrestling with that He is saying when, when, when?

GENTLENESS, mild, not strong or violent. To speak evil of no man, to be no brawlers but gentle, showing all meekness unto all men. **Titus 3:2** We at one time or another were disobedient to the ways of God, but the Christ in the person who witness to us drew us to the Lord with that loving kindness.

GOODNESS, moral excellence, virtuous behavior,... not knowing that the goodness of God leadeth thee to repentance? As we continue to do good eventually it subdues evil. That no matter what evil people may say about you or to you do not return evil for evil. But I say unto you, Love your enemies, bless them that curse you, do good to them that hate you, pray for them which despitefully use you and persecute you; That ye may be the children of your Father which is in heaven......... **Matthew 5:44,45.**

Remember we are the fruits of his seed, through the new birth of the Spirit, by the word of God, through his son Jesus Christ.

FAITH, complete acceptance of a truth which can not be demonstrated or proven by logical thought. Now faith is the substance of things hope for, the evidence of things not seen. Hebrews 11:6. We have to without a shadow of doubt believe in God based on his word.

I've heard so many times how we wait for the buses and trains to come and take us here and there we don't see them but we believe that they will come eventually.

We work all week long, sometimes two weeks before we get a pay check, but we believe that in that time frame we will eventually get paid. So why is it so hard for us to believe in God to do anything for us that we may ask in his will, and we receive it. We state by our

23

actions we're from Missouri you have to show me, but yet we don't see that bus or train or pay check but ye we believe, strange yes. But if we would take that same faith that we have in the physical and place that same faith into that of the spirit, we would see so much more of the manifestation of Gods power than ever before. Because what we must realize is that the things we receive from God are first created in the spirit and then manifested in the natural. Just as it was in the beginning.

MEEKNESS, humility, submissiveness. Who is a wise man and endued with knowledge among you? Let him show out of a good conversation his works with meekness of wisdom. **James 3:13** The wisdom given to us by God is not that of the world that we should boast in the flesh, but that which he gives us is to be able to acknowledge and recognize the tricks of the devil and not to succumb to them. Remember they are just tricks, there is no substance to what he says or the things that he tries to do. We have to be very careful as Jesus was in the wilderness when Satan used Gods word. **Luke 4:1-13** But his intentions were not that Jesus would obey God through the word, but that Jesus would obey Satan just because he used the word. And even today there are men and women of God who allow themselves to be used by Satan this way to keep Gods people in bondage. For they then begin to obey the creature instead of the Creator. He is just like a magician everything that he does is just an illusion, a form of reality and truth but not the real thing, a lie. And with the knowledge in which God has given unto us we are to use it wisely. And just as I have said, God gave this to us because it is his to give not ours. So we have to obey him in the use of it because he has the instructions on how it works, and the capability of its use.

<u>TEMPERANCE</u>, total abstinence from the desires and passions of the flesh....a lover of hospitality, a lover of good men, sober, just, holy, temperate; Holding fast the faithful words as he hath been taught, that he may be able by sound doctrine both to exhort and to convince the gainsayers. **Titus 1:8, 9**. We are to be the example to the world as to how God expects us to live in this life. We are to be transformed in our minds that the things our flesh had desired to do in the world must come under subjection to the word of God, for these things are pleasing to the flesh but are yet sinful. And in order for us to be a worshipers of Christ we must do so in spirit and in truth.

So now that we have presented our bodies unto God as a living sacrifice, holy and acceptable to God that we may prove that all we do is acceptable and the perfect will of God. **Romans 12:1, 2**

The Reaping

So as the crops are plentiful in time of harvest, so are the blessings of our reaping in the fields of righteousness. As in the time of Boaz and Ruth, when he told his people to glean the harvest so that some would be left for Ruth, she had not sown, planting the natural seed, but the things she had done for her mother-in-law Naomi in the spirit had now allowed Ruth to have favor with Boaz in the natural.

God also has favor with us. Blessed is the man that hearth me, watching daily at my gates, waiting at my doors. For who so findeth me, findeth life, and shall obtain favor of the Lord. Proverbs 8:34, 35. We know that if we seek those things of God and his righteousness that the things that we desire to have will be given unto us, but there are secret things God also desires to give us. The secret things belong unto the Lord our God: but those things which are revealed belong unto us and to our children forever, that we may do all the words of this law. **Deuteronomy 29:29**.

God not only wants to provide us with the natural and spiritual treasures but also of the physical. Our health is a basic necessity to our ministry, and living for God. Sickness is of the devil which is sin because **Isaiah 53:5** says.....with his stripes we are healed. We are not to give place to anything that's not like God. How can we go around laying hands on the sick and we still have illness in our bodies? How can we preach deliverance and we are still bound? How can we testify on what God can do, when we have not allowed him to do the things he says he can do in our lives. We are then an ineffective witness. We cannot tell of something that we have not experience for ourselves, or have come into the knowledge of.

God is our protection when the wiles of the devil begin to try to sift us as wheat. He that dwelleth in the secret place of the most high shall abide under the shadow of the Almighty. I will say of the Lord, He is my refuge and my fortress: my God; in him will I trust. Surely he shall deliver thee from the snare of the fowler, and from the noisome pestilence. He shall cover thee with his feathers, and under his wings shalt thou trust: his truth shall be thy shield and buckler. **Psalm 91:1-4**. God's word is our defense against the things of the enemy. When Jesus was in the wilderness and he was hungry because of his fasting. The devil suggested to Jesus that if he was the son of God that he should turn some stones into bread. But Jesus knew who the devil was and what his motive was. Jesus also knew who he was and because of that he did not need to prove himself to anyone.

And by him knowing who he was he was able to use that which had made him who he was, and that was the word of God.

....It is written, Man shall not live by bread alone, but by every word that proceedeth out of the mouth of God. **Matthew 4:4**. The weapon of our warfare is not carnal. We are to use the word of God to fight the battles. That is why Jesus stated that the battle was not ours but his. He is fighting the battle by us using him which is the word of God.

God is also a reviver. We become revived when his word is revealed though the Holy Spirit of revelation. **Ephesians 3:5** Which in other ages was not made known unto the sons of men, as it is now revealed unto his holy apostles and prophets by the Spirit; By us now knowing who God is in our lives, through his word we can now have the victory over all things pertaining to our life and the lives of our love ones and even our enemies.

O death, where is thy sting? O grave, where is thy victory? The sting of death is sin; and the strength of sin is the flesh. But thanks be to God, which giveth us the victory through our Lord Jesus Christ. Therefore my beloved brethren be ye steadfast, unmovable, always abounding in the work of the Lord, for as much as ye know that your labour is not in vain in the Lord. **1 Corinthians 15:55-58**.

The Conclusion

If my people, which are called by my name, shall humble themselves, and pray, seek my face and turn from their wicked ways; then will I hear from heaven, and will forgive their sins, and will heal their land. **2 Chronicles 7:14**

This word from God is so self-explanatory that only a fool would not be able to understand it. First of all being called by his name means that you have receive Jesus Christ in your life by repenting and being baptized in the name of Jesus. With the confessing with your mouth and believing in your heart that God raised Jesus Christ from the dead. Then receiving the gift of the promise which is the Holy Ghost. In being humble you allow the flesh to have no dominion over you. You then look to the Lord for that you stand in need of seek him, ask of him, Lord what would you have me to do and be, and pray, pray for families, pray for neighborhoods, pray for your pastors, pray for the Presidents, pray for your enemies, and most of all pray that the Lord have his way in your life.

Praying is our way of communicating with the Lord in having a relationship with Him. While you are doing that continue to stop doing the things that you use to do and want to do in the flesh. Then as we begin to have a relationship with the Lord the things we ask he will begin to grant unto us.

God desires that we have that relationship that we once had with Him in the Garden of Eden. When embarking on the Christian way of living will come against many obstacles and although they may seem to overwhelm us that we have no answer to the problems, and we have no explanation for the situations. God sees all and he has all the answers to any situation for all that will ever happen, for it has already happen in the word of God. Since we cannot know the time of the Lords' return, we have to be ready, for only God in his own wisdom knows the time and there is nothing anyone or anything that can change it. So we must continue to live as though Jesus is on his way at any time, which he is. God wants us to be busy laboring in the vineyard when he does come. We must not allow the enemy to distract us or discourage us from pressing toward the mark for the prize of the high calling of God in Christ Jesus.

Philippians 3:14 For I reckon that the sufferings of this present time are not worth to be compared with the glory which shall be revealed in us.

Romans 8:18 Blessed are they that do his commandments, that they may have right to the tree of life, and may enter in through the gates of the city. **Revelation 22:14.**

What a great day that will be!

Bonus

Poems

A Leaf Blowing in the Wind

As I sat gazing through the blinds of the window I said to
myself "I want to be like a leaf blowing in the Wind"!
The leaf has no decisions to make just to move
which ever way the Wind would blow.
Whether onto the rooftop or the street below, its
choice was to go where the Wind would blow.
To soar in the air or stay connected to the limb, its
choice was to go where the Wind would blow.
No worries, no concerns for the Wind knows
exactly where the leaf would be blown.
Carefree. Oblivious of time whether raked
into a pile or used as an arts and craft.
It didn't matter for it knows that where it came
from many more would follow……..

The Leaf Blowing In The Wind

New Skin

As I sat reading I glanced over to my hand
that I had some time ago burned.
But to my knowledge it had began to heal without
me having to apply any medicine to it.
As I took a closer look the top layer that we
call a scab was beginning to peel.
So I began to take it off and as I did so I began to see that the
old skin (scab) was hiding what I saw was the New Skin.
As I continued to take off the old skin the brilliance of the
New Skin shone was shiny and soft to the touch, brand new.
Just think if I had not of taken notice that the old skin was
coming off I would have never notice the **NEW SKIN**.

Refreshing Soul

As I stood with the water pulsating upon my
flesh it began to cry out for more.
It was something about my flesh that seemed
not to be able to get enough of water.
And then it dawned on me, Oh how my soul
thirsts for the presence of God.
How it can never get enough of Him.
Oh how it hungers and thirsts, wanting to
know more and more of Him.
Oh how it craves and desires as an addict craves
his addictions. I had to have Him.
But this flesh will one day have no need for water.
But even without the flesh I will always have a **Refreshing Soul**.

The Invited Guest

As I look through dark colored lens I wonder in my mind.
How can I go forward when all I can see is behind?
I question myself how did I get here? When had things changed?
The only things I remember are just faint in my mind.
I remember somewhat as I began to leave the house
how a small voice said to me stay and be my guest.
I ignored the voice saying it's my choice
so I left not obeying the voice.
On my way I stopped to asks some friends if
they wanted to ride, their response was no we're
resting our invited guest is going to arrive.
As I continued my quest I stopped at the store to pick up
some things that would make me feel at my best.
Still on my way I made another stop to the neighbor
man whose name I should not mention.
So, on the road I go to do what I want to do. Going
where I want to go and being who I want to be.
Not realizing that the weather had changed
and my speed limit was still the same.
I thought I had it all under control until I saw
myself no longer on that straight road.
Now in this place so dark and dreary, I ask myself, Am I dreaming?
I hear another voice saying **"The Invited Guest Has Arrived"**.

Reviews

"This book open my understanding about the importance of our Seed. God used this book to build my faith for the next step in my ministry. Thanks for being obedient to Gods voice."

-Charlotte Stephenson

"I can say every book I have read of hers has been powerful profound, and very revelatory. Very descriptive in what she wants you to see as you are reading the very scenery of her writing captivates the reader. It is not a boring reading but a read that will have you on edge for more and it will unction you to read scripture to seek out the mysteries of God"

-Taura Davis

Printed in the United States
By Bookmasters